Art Works

Drawing sters

Carolyn Scrace

SCRIBBLERS

Author:
Carolyn Scrace graduated from Brighton
College of Art, UK, with a focus on design
and illustration. She has since worked in
animation, advertising and children's
publishing. She has a special interest in
natural history and has written many books
on the subject, including *Lion Journal* and
Gorilla Journal in the *Animal Journal* series.

How to use this book:

Follow the easy, numbered instructions.
Simple step-by-step stages enable
budding young artists to create their
own amazing drawings.

What you will need:

1. Paper.
2. Wax crayons.
3. Felt-tip pens to add colour.

Published in Great Britain in MMXV by
Scribblers, a division of Book House
25 Marlborough Place, Brighton BN1 1UB
www.salariya.com
www.book-house.co.uk

ISBN-13: 978-1-910184-84-4

A CIP catalogue record for this book is available
from the British Library.

Printed and bound in China.

Contents

Sparks!

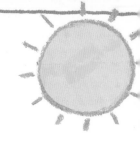

1 Sparks needs a head,

2 ...a short body with two legs,

3 ...two arms and hands,

4 ...two feet,

5 ...three big round eyes, a tiny nose and spiky hair!

6 Now draw in his big mouth with pointed teeth.

4

Use crayons to add colour and some monster spots all over Sparks's face, body, legs and feet.

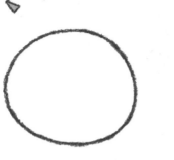

Snips!

1 Snips needs a body,

2 ...four legs and feet,

3 ...and four more legs and feet!

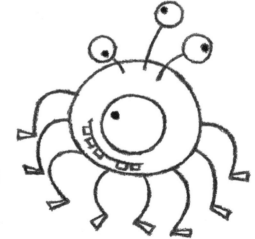

4 Now draw in one **big** eye,

5 ...a mouth and teeth,

6 ...and her three wobbly eyes on stalks!

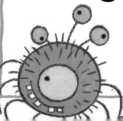

Draw in thin lines to make Snips's body hairy.

Colour in with felt-tip pens.

7

Widget!

1 Widget needs a body,

2 ...a head,

3 ...two arms and hands,

4 ...two legs and feet!

5 Now draw in two big ears and a nose,

6 ...two eyes, a mouth and teeth!

8

Use a crayon to colour the inside shape of Widget's ears.

Colour in with felt-tip pens.

Add some pointy scales to Widget's body,

...and her beautiful curly tail!

9

 # Chisel!

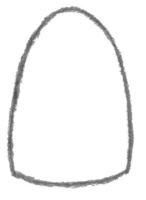  

1 Chisel needs a body, 2 ...a head, 3 ...two legs and feet,

4 ...two long arms and hands,

5 ...and a **big** mouth and teeth!

6 Now draw one big eye and his tiny horns!

Use a white crayon to add stripes to Chisel's body.

Colour in with felt-tip pens.

11

Rasp!

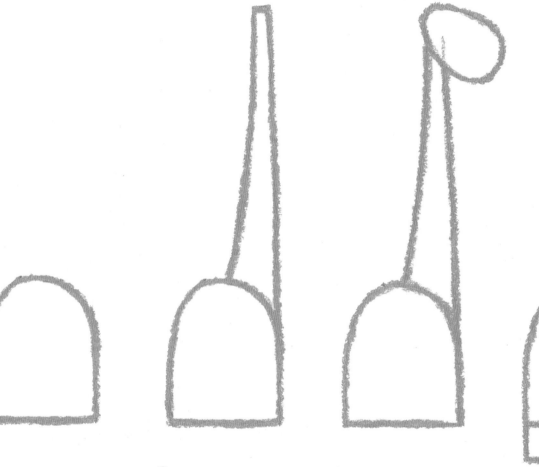

1 Rasp needs a body,

2 ...a very **long** neck,

3 ...a head,

4 ...two feet,

12

Horn

Draw in a zigzag shape all the way down the back of Rasp's body.

Colour in with felt-tip pens.

5 ...and two arms and hands.

6 Draw in two eyes, a horn and his big smile.

 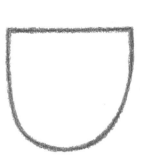 # Mallet!

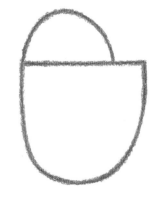

1 Mallet needs
a body,

2 ...a head,

3 ...two legs and feet,

4 ...two arms
and hands,

5 ...a tail,

6 ...an eye, a nose and
a **big** mouth!

Draw in lots of pointed teeth!

Add spots to Mallet's body and tail with a crayon.

Colour in with felt-tip pens.

15

Plug!

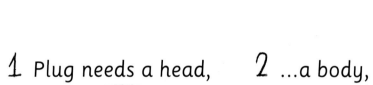

1 Plug needs a head,

2 ...a body,

3 ...three legs and feet,

3 ...and two arms and hands.

5 Now add her eyes, nose and a big mouth,

6 ...with **lots** of teeth!

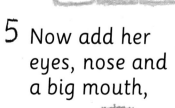

Horns

Draw in Plug's
two ears and two
sharp horns.

Now add spots
to her face.

Colour in with
felt-tip pens.

17

Spanner!

1 Spanner needs a head,

2 ...a body,

Stalks

3 ...two legs, feet and a tail,

4 ...and **four** arms and hands.

5 Now draw in Spanner's big eyes on stalks,

6 ...and her nose, mouth and teeth!

Use a crayon to add spots to Spanner's face, body and tail.

Colour in with felt-tip pens.

19

 # Bolt!

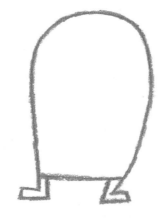

1 Bolt needs a body,

2 ...two small legs and feet,

3 ...two big arms and hands,

5 ...a very **big** mouth and teeth!

4 Draw in two eyes, a nose,

6 ...and his two horns.

Draw in spots on Bolt's body, arms and hands and stripes on his horns.

Colour in with felt-tip pens.

Clamp!

1 Clamp needs a head,

2 ...a body,

3 ...two legs and feet,

4 ...two arms and hands,

5 ...two eyes and one long nose like an elephant's trunk!

6 Add his mouth and teeth.

Colour in with
felt-tip pens.

Use a crayon
to draw stripes
on his body.

Draw in Clamp's tail.

23

Putty!

1 Putty needs **two** heads,

2 ...a body,

3 ...**two** necks, two legs and feet,

4 ...two arms and hands,

5 ...and **one** tail!

6 Draw a big eye on each of her heads.

Draw in Putty's mouth and teeth and add a zigzag pattern to her body and tail.

Colour in with felt-tip pens.

25

Pincer!

1 Pincer needs a head,

2 ...a wiggly body,

3 ...two arms and hands,

4 ...and **lots** of legs and feet!

5 Draw in two eyes and horns,

6 ...and her long nose and teeth.

Draw in Pincer's antennae!

antennae

Add stripes to her horns and body using crayons.

Colour in with felt-tip pens.

27

Nut!

1 Nut needs a **big** head,

2 ...a **small** body,

3 ...two legs and feet,

4 ...and two long arms and hands.

5 Add two big eyes, a nose and mouth,

6 ...and two antennae!

Draw in Nut's sharp teeth and finish off his eyes.

Use crayons to add spots to Nut's head and stripes to his body.

Colour in with felt-tip pens.

29

Sprocket!

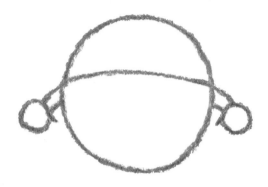

1 Sprocket needs a **fat** body,

2 ...a **huge** mouth,

3 ...two tiny arms and hands,

4 ...two legs and feet,

5 ...and two **extra** legs and feet!

6 Now draw in one eye, his teeth and two antennae!

Colour in with felt-tip pens.

31

glossary

Antennae stalks or feelers that grow on the heads of some animals.

Eyestalk a movable stalk with an eye on top.

Horn a hard, bony spike that grows out of an animal's head. Some animals use their horns to defend themselves from attack.

Scales small, hard plates that cover and protect the bodies of some animals.

Tail the back part of an animal that helps it balance.

index